STRESS FREE TRAVEL

TIPS & IDEAS

For

SENIORS

And Those Traveling With

SPECIAL NEEDS

Meredith "Kit" Bromfield M.A.Ed

Special Section By
Ian Sandage, Nutritionist

ISBN: 9781796594171

Printed in the United States of America

For permission to use material, contact:
Meredith Kit Bromfield
www.cbgt.com
www.meredithbromfield.com
(630) 618-9400

This is book is dedicated to my grandson,

Logan Daniel

DISCLAIMER

The information presented in this entire book is to be used solely for informational purposes only. The author or any other parties or companies mentioned in this book are not liable for any advice given, websites visit or transactions made. The author makes no representations or warranties with respect to any information offered or provided on or through this book or websites mentioned. The author is not liable for any direct or indirect claim, loss or damage resulting from use of this book or any web site(s) linked to/from it.

TABLE OF CONTENTS

DECISIONS

DECISIONS

DECISIONS

DECIDE WHERE YOU WANT TO GO

What kind of trip will this be?

- ❖ Adventure
- ❖ Celebrating a significant event (birthday, anniversary, honeymoon, marriage)
- ❖ Cultural
- ❖ Educational
- ❖ Food themed
- ❖ Historical venue
- ❖ Leisure
- ❖ Giving Back - Make a Difference
- ❖ Movie themed (i.e. Sound of Music)
- ❖ Places on my bucket list
- ❖ Medical (people travel to other countries for surgeries & dental procedures)
- ❖ Religious
- ❖ Revisiting a site that has significant meaning
- ❖ Ancestry Tour
- ❖ Spa & Wellness
- ❖ Wineries

Once you have made these decisions, then this is where the real planning begins.

You will need to ask yourself the following questions:

- ❖ How much time will you need to visit these places?

- ❖ Are they places that are major tourist attractions?

- ❖ Are they off the grid? Places off the grid may need more planning than visiting major tourist attractions.

- ❖ Who do you need to contact to set up the trips?

- ❖ Can you navigate setting them up by yourself?

- ❖ Who do you want to travel with?

- ❖ When do you want to go?

- ❖ What is your budget for this trip?

- ❖ Do you need travel insurance to cover the trip?

- ❖ What about vaccinations?

- ❖ Is this place dangerous to travel to at this time?

- ❖ Will you need a visa or will a passport do?

- ❖ Are there tours that visit all the places you want to see?

❖ Can you have someone create a personalized tour for you for part or all of your trip?

❖ Do you like to travel with friends?

❖ Are you up for meeting new people when you travel?

❖ Are you physically able to visit every site? Some sites may require excessive walking or traversing some very hazardous areas. I find that when people visit other countries, that oftentimes the terrain is difficult to navigate for seniors.

❖ Would you consider staying in someone's home when you travel?

❖ Do you have dietary restrictions that would curtail visiting certain places?

❖ Do you have a medical condition that needs to have you near a medical facility when you travel?

Where will you find out all this information? This will be addressed in the following chapters.

WHAT DO YOU WANT TO SEE

Are you interested in the specifics of the area: culture, food, activities, or?

Are you an historical buff and seeing places that are significant in history is important to you?

Bottom line is what is your dream list for what you want to see or do?

For example, if you were interested in historic sites in France, you might want to visit the following:

- ❖ Palace of Versailles
- ❖ Nimes Arena–Roman amphitheatre 1st century BC
- ❖ Somme battlefields
- ❖ Notre Dame Cathedral of Paris
- ❖ The Eiffel Tower
- ❖ Pont du Gard Ancient Roman bridge & aqueduct
- ❖ Carcassonne created in 6th century BC
- ❖ Les Invalides completed in Nov 24, 1670
- ❖ Sainte Chapelle 1246 built by King Louis IX
- ❖ Pere Lachaise Cemetery established in 1804 by Napoleon

Do you enjoy visiting new and exotic places?

SOME PLACES YOU MIGHT WANT TO VISIT

- ❖ Abu Dhabi
- ❖ Alberobello, Italy
- ❖ Albuquerque, New Mexico
- ❖ Angel Falls, Venezuela
- ❖ Bali
- ❖ Bangkok, Thailand
- ❖ Bayreuth, Germany
- ❖ Big Sur, California
- ❖ Boise, Idaho
- ❖ Brussels, Belgium
- ❖ Buenos Aries, Argentina
- ❖ Cancun Underwater Museum
- ❖ Columbia Pacific Coast
- ❖ Copenhagen, Denmark
- ❖ Deans Bue Hole, Bahamas
- ❖ Edmonton, Alberta
- ❖ Egypt
- ❖ Greenland
- ❖ Grenada

- ❖ Icehotel, Jukkasjarvi, Sweden
- ❖ Ija Valley Japan
- ❖ Ireland
- ❖ Isuzu Falls, Argentina
- ❖ Ithaa Undersea restaurant, Maldives
- ❖ Jordan
- ❖ Las Pozas Xilitia, Mexico a 20 acre fantasyland
- ❖ Los Cabos, Mexico
- ❖ Luang Prabang, Laos
- ❖ Mauritius
- ❖ Mendoza, Argentina
- ❖ Mexico City, Mexico
- ❖ Mont St. Michel, France
- ❖ Montenegro
- ❖ Moranington Peninsula, Australia
- ❖ Namibia Lakes, Australia
- ❖ New Orleans, Louisiana
- ❖ Pamukkale Thermal Pools, Turkey
- ❖ Pancake Rocks, New Zealand
- ❖ Pjeongchange, So Korea
- ❖ Plitvice Lakes National Park, Croatia

- ❖ Puerto-Princesa Subterranean River, Philippines
- ❖ Saliva Island, Italy
- ❖ San Antonio, Texas
- ❖ Sao Paulo, Brazil
- ❖ Shanghai, China
- ❖ Sichuan, China
- ❖ Skellig Michael island, Ireland
- ❖ Slovenia
- ❖ Solta, Croatia
- ❖ Southern Sri Lanka
- ❖ Tel Aviv, Israel
- ❖ The Bahamas
- ❖ The Berkshires, Massachusetts
- ❖ The Peloponnese, Greece
- ❖ Toronto, Canada
- ❖ Uzbekistan
- ❖ Valletta, Malta
- ❖ Washington DC
- ❖ Zambia
- ❖ Fuji

I hope this gives you some ideas of places to add to your bucket list. There are places all over the world for you to explore and see!

Sometimes the most interesting things that we encounter are not even what were expected.

I would like to share my high tea story.

I was in Lake Wanaka, New Zealand. My daughter and I saw an advertisement for a high tea being held in the area. As we both loved high teas and had experienced it in London, Victoria, and Chicago, we thought it might be fun to do one in New Zealand.

Neither one of us had the type of clothing that usually was appropriate for a high tea so we questioned if it was ok to attend.

We set up a time to be picked up for this event. We were assured that casual attire was acceptable and were told that comfortable shoes were important.

We were picked up and driven to a pier where a small craftsman boat was waiting for us. We were the only 2 people who went on the boat. There were some concerns shared between my daughter and I as no one else was with us and the boat seemed really small.

We went to an island where the driver ran the boat aground, and we were told to get off the boat. No pier and still no other people. It was there that we started a hike up a small mountain. Still no hotel or structure where a tea would be held was visible. The whole time my daughter and I were concerned what was happening and where we were going.

We finally made it to the top of this mountain, and the view was absolutely amazing. It was at that time that our guide pulled out a thermos of tea and a Tupperware container filled with chocolate chip cookies.

We had high tea! Thinking back to my trip to New Zealand, it was truly one of the highlights.

Do you have a specific travel dream that you feel may not be possible?

I would like to share one of those dreams of one of my clients. This person's dream was to have a pool wedding on a cruise ship.   This individual came to me with this request. He was confined to a wheel chair but could stand when in water, and he wanted to say his vows standing.

My response was let me see what I can do for you. I contacted every cruise line and all said no except 2. One of the ships said it would be a maybe that they would consider after I booked the cruise, but this made me concerned because they would not guarantee this. The other cruise line Princess agreed to allow a pool wedding.

I am glad to report that not only did the captain officiate at the pool wedding, but he actually stopped the ship because the waves were high.

So whatever your dream is, there just might be a chance to make it come true.

Is there something on your bucket list that seems impossible? Maybe it isn't. Maybe there is a creative way to accomplish what it is you want to do.

Write it down:

Now contact a Travel Advisor and see what magic they can do to help you make your dream come true.

BEST TIME TO TRAVEL

What is important to you when you travel?

Do you mind lots of people everywhere you go?

Do you want to be a part of a special event? Olympics? Rio's Mardi Gras? Or something else?

If looking to travel and not having a specific event you want to attend, then I would suggest traveling during the collar seasons April/May and Sept/Oct. They are my personal favorites.

There are reasons for this:

- Better rates

  For Alaska you can save up to $500 per person for cruises.

  If traveling to Alaska, consider the Northbound in April–May and the Southbound in September-October.

- Less people visiting the sites with a few exceptions:

  Japan-cherry blossom festival

  Stay away from holidays, spring break and special events regional to that area you are interested in visiting.

HOW DO YOU WANT TO TRAVEL

Ok now you know what you want to see or do. Next determine what will be the best mode of transportation to this location. In some cases your choices will be limited.

Every transportation option has benefits and drawbacks and knowing what those are will help you in determining which is the best way to travel.

Airplane – the fastest way to get to a location. You are bound by the time schedule, and may not have an airport close to the location you want. Delays, security checks, uncomfortable seats and other issues can occur when you fly. If you fly frequently, I would encourage you to become pre-TSA approved. You can go to a local office and register; the cost is currently $85 per person and good for 10 years. This allows you to bypass the security lines where you have to take off your coat and shoes and take out your liquids, and is the best way to get through airport security. If you need any help when arriving at the airport, make arrangements prior to your flights. It makes flying a lot less stressful.

Train – you are limited to where the train goes. Trains can provide a comfortable ride and one that allows you to view your surroundings without having to drive. Please note that trains can be expensive especially in certain areas and at certain times of the year. If you are traveling at night, a sleeper car would be a good choice. Europe by rail is awesome. Book first class whenever you can as the upgrade is definitely worth the extra cost.

Bus - sitting for long hours may be a challenge if you have any health concerns. You are at the mercy of the bus driver and their schedule. It would be considered one of the most economical ways to travel.

Car – you are in control but you also have to accept all the challenges of driving yourself. If you are visiting areas that are unfamiliar, it could cause undue stress. Another thing is you may miss sites and information because you have to focus on driving.

Private Driver – it can be expensive if it is only two of you traveling or a single person, as the rates are based on the time and distance. One way to minimize that is to have more people in your group traveling with you. This is an amazing way to see multiple out of the way locations and have someone tell you about things that you normally would not have seen or done.

I remember one such group. There were 5 of us, and we hired a driver to take us to Pompeii and the Amalfi Coast. It was a grand adventure, filled with many amazing insights of the area and the sites. On the way back, we were entertained by our driver singing Italian songs. This was a memorable experience that only would have happened in this type of setting.

Tour Group – this can be a combination of bus, boat, and/or plane depending on what and where you are going. The benefit is all challenges are someone else's responsibility. Every detail is handled in advance including meals, sights seen, and travel arrangements.

In some cases they will even hold your passports as you go from one location to the next insuring that you will not forget or lose it.

This can be a wonderful experience if you are traveling with great people and knowledgeable guides. If not, it can be a really long and boring trip.

River Boat Cruise – great way to see certain towns and cities especially in Europe. There are many different cruise lines vying for your business. Viking is the most known, but there are other ones like AmaWaterways, Avalon, Amadeus, Uniworld just to name a few. These others are European owned and cater to Europeans whereas Viking targets Americans only. You need to check all costs as some include all tours and others do not. The more you know the better for you. Also you will want to know what their policies are when the rivers are low. How do they handle this? Some will give you a full refund while others will just bus you to the next location. These are just some of the things to consider when looking into this mode of travel.

Cruise ship – allows going to areas that would be expensive to fly to. Another great advantage is that you pack and unpack only once and experience new places at every port. Best value for travel choice.

Drawback is that you are limited to where the cruise line goes to. Additional costs of tours, gratuities, wifi need to be looked at when determining whether this is the best value. This is a leisure way of traveling for seniors. If cruising is something you are considering and want to get the best value, then I would recommend that you stick with one cruise line. The advantage of being loyal to a single cruise line is in the rewards. Once you reach a certain level with the cruise line, preferred boarding, special cocktail parties, and other amenities are there for you and your guests.

Tour Group

If you have a specific area that you want to visit and a group takes care of all the details, this can be your best choice. There are several levels of service that various tour groups offer, from luxury to budget. Usually you will see the difference in the hotels that are booked, meals served and any amenities added. If this is a choice, look at what is important to you. Does it make a difference if you are in a 3 star or in a 4 star hotel? In the final analysis, if you want to have someone else take care of all of your details and schedule all the various sites, this is a good choice. One cautionary note is if you are on a bus tour, be prepared to sit on a bus for 4 to 5 hours almost every day.

Customized Trip

Here is where you have your travel advisor take care of all of your desires and customizes your trip including air, transfers, hotels, and special events.

Your Advisor can arrange for private limo services for you to visit specific cities or sites. The cost can be much higher, but you can minimize this by having more than one person share your ride.

I had a client who wanted to visit a town he had been to when he was in the war that had a population of only 300 people. I set up a private limo to get him there.

Form Your Own Group

There are lots of perks for your own group, which include private tours, special places that are only accessible by small group. Usually groups are considered 8 people or more but not always; it depends on various factors. As a side note regarding cruises, if you book a group with a cruise line, and only two of you end up actually travelling, you are still entitled to the same perks allocated for your group. Cruises consider five or more cabins as a group.

BUDGETS

&

DISCOUNTS

WHAT IS YOUR BUDGET?

There are many ways to travel that fit everyone's budget, but you have to determine what yours is.

The question is what is more important, comfort or cost?

There are economical ways to travel all over the world if you make certain concessions. For example staying in off-the-way locations rather than in the heart of a city can garner lower rates on hotels.

Have you considered a Bed and Breakfast, senior hostels, or even exchange homes?

What about locations that are known for lower rates on food, hotels and attractions?

One of those areas is the Far East, Thailand, Viet Nam; they offer amazing places without the higher price tags. Portugal has better rates than Spain. There are many places that are not well known tourist spots that will have great rates and allow you to really immerse yourself in the culture. The challenge is because these are not well known locations, many tour groups will not offer them to you.

Here is where you form your own small group – hire a driver for the duration of your stay in that location and truly enjoy the adventure. I did this once in Boston. A friend and I rented a limo driver for 4 hours; the cost was $200. This person basically took us to all the sites in Boston and because we arrived in a limo, people thought we were famous or something and were treated to some amazing experiences. This option is available all over the world. The price can seem like sticker shock initially, but consider that you are paying for the vehicle and the driver and it doesn't matter if there are 2 people or 10. The more people you have to share the cost, the more affordable the trip becomes.

Have you considered taking a class that includes a trip? I took an online course of the history and geography of Israel which included a trip to Israel. It was one of the most amazing trips I have ever taken.

Should I do something or see something when I travel? My hard and fast rule is: I may never get to this place again to do these activities. I will not allow the cost to determine whether I do this activity or not.

DISCOUNTS

WAYS TO SAVE MONEY WHEN YOU TRAVEL

Remember the rule of flying on Tuesdays, Wednesdays and Saturdays. This will garner you the cheapest flights.

Demand drives prices up – most people travel Thursday, Friday, Sunday and Monday.

Note if you find a good price grab it – if you wait, it will probably be gone at a later time. I had a client who wanted a business class airfare Chicago to Tel Aviv; the price was $3900. The client was not sure so he wanted to wait. The next day the same class fare was $6500 for the same flight, and two days later it was $8300.

Hit the shoulder season if you can when traveling

Southern Hemisphere

- ✓ High season is late November until after Easter
- ✓ Low season is May to November

Northern Hemisphere

- ✓ High season is May to late September
- ✓ Low season is October to April

Be a little impulsive

Sign up for your favorite airline's email list to be alerted for last minute specials.

Check out Groupon or Living Social for luxurious planned getaways for a fraction of normal price.

Look into less popular cities and/or countries

- ✓ i.e. rather than Aspen to ski, look into Lake Tahoe, Nevada or Brian Head, Utah
- ✓ look into traveling to Portugal versus Spain

Ditch the hotel

Look into Airbnb (short term house rentals) or VRBO (lots more options, beach house, condo, cabin to mention only a few). Look into sites offering house sitting or pet sitting, exchanging homes.

Get off the plane

If the airline needs a seat, volunteer yours.

Usually they will put you on a later flight that same day plus give you a voucher for a free future flight. If you do have to stay overnight to catch a flight the next day, they will give you vouchers for hotel and meals.

Saving money on food

Brown bag it (i.e. buy a subway sandwich eat ½ in the airport and the other ½ on the plane)

Check out local grocery stores rather than eating out all the time

Hydrate on the cheap

Bring an empty water bottle with you through security (most airports have fill stations throughout the airport). This will save you a $4 bottle of water.

Find new ways to get around

Look into public transportation (train, bus, Uber, Lyft).

Be aware that in some cities Uber and Lyft cannot pick up at the airport. Check out Google maps and Citymapper with your destinations and look up schedules for trains and busses. Print out a map of the route - look into subway, monorail or bus instead of taxi.

Look for hotels in locations that put you near many of the attractions that you are interested in visiting. You could actually walk to them. It may cost a little bit more for the lodging, but you might save lots in transportation costs to the attraction.

Take a cue from extreme couponers

There are coupons for literally everything.

Take advantage of 1st time customers.

Apps like Groupon and Living Social have deals for activities and food that cut costs.

Book directly

Airlines often offer more flexibility and cheaper flights than 3rd party sellers (i.e. Expedia). Also look into websites like Skyscanner or Google Flights to possibly find cheaper flights than going to the airline directly.

When booking a package with tour groups or cruises, take advantage of their flights. Because they block a large number of seats, they usually have the best prices for those flights.

When in doubt Ask for discounts

Check AARP versus Senior versus best rate.

Look into senior discounts on transportation, tours, accommodations and dining reservations.

Create a senior group

Ask for group discounts and added perks such as private tours or activities while traveling.

TRAVELING
BY
AIR

TRAVELING BY AIR

- ❖ Book a non-stop flight to your destination as often as you can.
- ❖ Arrange for Transportation Inside the Airport.
- ❖ Check with your airline about their boarding policies for those with disabilities.
- ❖ Be sure to reserve any special services needed when booking your flight.
- ❖ Select an Aisle Seat on Long Flights.
- ❖ If you are traveling with a companion have seats across from each other.
- ❖ Delta is the best for traveling long distance if you want to have 2 seats to yourself.
- ❖ Look into airlines that are off the grid – Singapore, Emirates, Qatar, Japan Airlines, Air New Zealand, Virgin Air. They offer the best service – the seats are roomier, and in some cases actually may be less expensive.
- ❖ If traveling with any disabilities, make sure you or your travel agent has contacted the airline.

Tips and tricks all travelers should know

THERE ARE WAYS TO GET MORE COMFORTABLE AIRLINE SEATS:

Avoid "low cost" carriers. Allegiant, Frontier, and Spirit have reputations for small seats & scarcity of personal space.

Look for good seats in economy, but be prepared to pay for those seats.

The exit row and bulkhead seats typically have more room than a standard seat, if you can afford them. The worst seats are the ones in the rear of the aircraft, which don't recline. There are exceptions and you might want to ask before you book to see if those seats do recline. I recently flew to Israel on United and my travel companion and I had the 2 last seats. The seats did recline, and they gave me extra room to store things on the floor next to me because I was seated behind three seats. Also there was room behind my seat for my extra stuff.

Travel with pillows and blankets. There are blankets on long overseas flights but usually are very thin. Carrying donuts or a trtl (pronounced "turtle") with you for your neck and head is also a good idea.

To get an aisle seat:

Ask for it.

If you have a loyalty card, you may be entitled to a better seat, even if you're sitting in economy class.

Pay for it. This is especially important on long flights. It will definitely be worth it for your comfort.

WRITING AN AIRLINE CONSUMER COMPLAINT LETTER

Be precise. Include details such as your confirmation code, flight number and travel date.

Explain in simple, non-dramatic terms exactly what happened that has caused you this inconvenience. I recently was on a flight that ended up being cancelled after having a 6 hour delay and after having boarded the plane and enduring another delay before we were told the flight was cancelled. One of my fellow passengers had a connecting flight the following day and had to book with another airline, and the cost was an additional $650. This all needed to be indicated in the letter.

Explain what it is you want. As in the case of my friend, he wanted the entire cost of the additional flight reimbursed, plus a voucher for another flight on this airline carrier. Everyone staying with the original airline did receive vouchers for hotel and meals because another flight on this carrier was not available until the next day. He felt he was also entitled to this same hotel/meal vouchers even though he was switching carriers.

BE SPECIFIC TO WHAT IT IS YOU WANT:

Are you asking them to refund your checked bag fee?

To add miles to your frequent-flyer account

To simply apologize

To give you a voucher for a future flight

To pay for any additional costs that occurred because of their delay.

Address the letter to personnel in the complaint department.

Once you hear from the airlines, if it is not resolved to your liking, your next step is to call the airline directly and ask to speak to a supervisor. Again state your case and indicate how the airline can fix your situation. Emphasize that your willingness to fly this airline in the future may be dependent upon satisfactory solution to your concern.

Three things airlines won't tell you about vouchers:

They are legally required to offer you cash. In some cases, such as a canceled flight, an airline is required to offer you a refund. In every instance, they will try to offer you the option to rebook the flight or accept a voucher for a future flight.

Because of blackout dates, it may make it impossible to redeem the voucher for the time frames that you want to travel in. Always read the fine print on the voucher before you agree to it. If you don't like the terms, ask for a better deal, or a refund.

Vouchers will expire sooner than you think. Most vouchers last far less than a year from the date of your aborted trip.

My husband's voucher with Frontier Airlines was only good for 3 months.

How to handle a rude TSA agent:

Report the agent to a supervisor.

Ask for a Supervisory Transportation Security Officer (STSO) immediately.

Complain in writing.

Email directly to the TSA (tsa.gov/contact-center/form/complaints).

Contact your elected representative because TSA agents are federal employees.

You will find email addresses for your representative at house.gov/representatives/find. Congress

How to avoid an in-flight emergency:

Avoid flying if you're sick, recovering from a serious illness or have a condition that is easily exacerbated by the stress of flying.

Don't fly if you're contagious. Contact the Airlines and ask them to issue a credit and waive the change fee. They will require some medical form stating what it is you have.

If at all possible, avoid late night flights. They have an increased chance of delays.

How to avoid flights from hell:

Fly nonstop and avoid connecting flights.

Opt for earlier flights rather than late night flights.

Know your rights, all spelled out in the "**DOT's Fly Rights Brochure**," which is available online.

When you travel understand that things can go wrong from time to time. Getting stressed out and angry is not going to fix the situation or make it go away. Relax, have a drink and realize that this is all part of the travel experience.

How to get around the new carry-on rules:

Fit it all into your "personal" bag. That's defined as a shoulder bag, purse, laptop bag, backpack, or other small suitcase that is 9 inches x 10 inches x 17 inches or less.

Use a luggage shipping service. Companies such as Luggage Forward and many other similar services will send your bags ahead of you for a price.

You want to be one of the first to board to insure that overhead space is available for your carry-on bag. Boarding is by zone. Buying an upgraded seat will get you a higher boarding zone number.

If your bag is too big or overhead space is not available, in some cases the airline will check it for FREE, but this is not a guarantee, and it could cost a premium for your luggage.

 ## WHAT TO BRING ON A PLANE

Customize this list to your specific needs. Check off any item you feel you may need with you on the plane.

Items bolded are a must.

- ☐ Addresses for postcards
- ☐ Airborne or vitamin C
- ☐ Antacid tablets
- ☐ Antihistamine tables for allergies
- ☐ ATM card
- ☐ Binoculars for sightseeing
- ☐ Camera and spare batteries, charger and spare memory cards
- ☐ Candied ginger for motion sickness
- ☐ Cash
- ☐ Chewing gum or hard candies
- ☐ Compact hi-speed portable phone charger as many of the terminals at the airport may be already in use. Besides being portable, you don't have to be seated next to an outlet.

- ☐ Complete information to refill prescription drugs
- ☐ **Compression stockings or wool socks**
- ☐ Contact information for all doctors
- ☐ Contact lens case
- ☐ **Copies of all important documents (e.g. passport, driver's license, prescriptions, credit cards)**
- ☐ **Credit cards – VISA is the best known**
- ☐ Diarrhea tablets
- ☐ Doctor's authorization for prescription drug
- ☐ **Driver's license**
- ☐ Ear buds
- ☐ **Emergency contact information for the people back home**
- ☐ **Empty water bottle through security and fill it once you pass**
- ☐ Entertainment options (e.g. playing cards, crossword puzzles, games, music, movies)
- ☐ **Epinephrine**
- ☐ E-reader and charger
- ☐ Eye drops

- ☐ Eye Glass case

- ☐ Eye mask

- ☐ First aid kit

- ☐ Foreign language phrasebooks

- ☐ **Foreign currency for tips**–get it at your local bank (when I arrived in Israel, the place for exchanging money had run out of money).

- ☐ Game console/player and charger

- ☐ Gas relief tablets

- ☐ Guidebooks

- ☐ Hand sanitizers (gel or wipes)

- ☐ Headphones instead for anyone who wears hearing aids

- ☐ Information for embassies and consulates at your destination

- ☐ **Information for hotels en route to your destination (connecting airports in cities you'll pass through)**

- ☐ **Information for local hospitals at your destination**

- ☐ **Information for reporting lost or stolen credit cards**

- ☐ **Insurance details (e.g. travel, medical, car, credit card)**
- ☐ **Itinerary**
- ☐ Laptop and charger
- ☐ **Light jacket or blanket**
- ☐ Magnifying glass
- ☐ Maps and directions
- ☐ Medical and vaccination records
- ☐ **MEDICATIONS/PRESCRIPTION DRUGS**
- ☐ Mild laxative tablets
- ☐ **Mobile phone and charger**
- ☐ **Money belt or fanny pack**
- ☐ **Neck brace for long flights** (my favorite is a TRTL – recommended by chiropractors)
- ☐ Pain, fever relief, and cold tablets
- ☐ **Passport**
- ☐ **Photos of your luggage** (for identification purposes if it is lost or delayed)
- ☐ Portable oxygen concentrator
- ☐ Portable wheelchair
- ☐ Power converter/electrical socket adapters

- ☐ Power cords, connection cables, spare batteries
- ☐ Prepaid phone cards
- ☐ Preparation H wipes
- ☐ **Reading material**
- ☐ Sinus medication Spray or tablets)
- ☐ Sleep-aid medication
- ☐ Small flashlight/reading light
- ☐ **Snacks**
- ☐ Spare batteries for hearing aids
- ☐ Spare pair of contact lenses
- ☐ **Spare pair of glasses**
- ☐ **Sunglasses**
- ☐ **Sweater or Cashmere pashmina scarves (as planes can be cold)**
- ☐ Tablet and charger
- ☐ Tissues
- ☐ **Travel confirmations and reservations**
- ☐ Travel journal
- ☐ Vitamins

MAKE ARRANGEMENTS TO GET TO THE AIRPORT

❖ If flying out of DIA – the Hilton Garden will allow you to leave your car with them up to 15 days if you stay there the night before your flight. They will also shuttle you to and from the airport.

❖ Consider hiring a limo to take you to the airport. **www.accarol.com** is great in the Tri-Lakes Area.

DAY YOU ARE TRAVELING

❖ Wear Loose Clothing (sweats are great for traveling).

❖ Get to the airport early - 3 hours before your flight for international and 2 hours for domestic.

NAVIGATE THE AIRPORT WITH EASE

- ❖ Take advantage of the assistance offered at the airport.
- ❖ Look into having someone drive you to the airport rather than you drive and park.
- ❖ Arrange for a wheelchair or assistance ahead of time if needed.
- ❖ Delta Airlines will help through check-in with 48 hours notice of your flight.
- ❖ American Airlines provides special assistance to passengers with disabilities.
- ❖ Hire an independent company like <u>Royal Airport Concierge Services</u>, who will meet anyone who needs help at the curb to help them check their bags and escort them to security. They typically charge $150 to $250 and serve dozens of airports across the U.S.

GOING THROUGH SECURITY

- ❖ All U.S. airports offer expedited screening to passengers 75 and older.
- ❖ SIGN UP FOR PRE-TSA $85 AND LASTS 10 YEARS.
- ❖ Pre-TSA approval allows one to move through security without removing shoes or jacket or their liquids bag, and many airports have lanes specifically for use by passengers with disabilities and medical conditions so they don't have to wait in line.
- ❖ Have all medication in one plastic bag separate from their liquids.
- ❖ All liquid containers must be 3.4oz or less and must be placed in a one-quart size clear plastic zip-top bag with only one bag per passenger allowed.

ONCE ON THE PLANE

* Skip the alcohol and drink lots of water.

* Bring a water bottle with you on the plane. This will allow you to make sure you stay hydrated on your flight. Dehydration is the single most important thing to try and prevent when flying.

* **DON'T BE AFRAID TO ASK CREW MEMBERS FOR HELP.**

* **HAVE HEALTHY SNACKS** (nuts, sliced fruit, energy bars are all good options) pack in zip lock bag and add some wet wipes.

* **STAND UP AND STRETCH OFTEN** (after sitting for every 50 minutes, get up and move).

GETTING OFF THE PLANE

* Ask for help with your Luggage.

* Wait till everyone gets off before you deplane. In that way, you can have a flight attendant help you.

TRAVELING BY BOAT

RIVER BOAT CRUISE:

This is a great way to see certain towns and cities especially in Europe. There are many different cruise lines vying for your business. Viking is the most known, but there are other ones like AmaWaterways, Avalon, Amadeus, and Uniworld just to name a few. These others are European owned and cater to Europeans whereas Viking targets Americans only. You need to check all costs as some include all tours and others do not. The more you know the better for you. Also you will want to know what their policies are when the rivers are low. How do they handle this? Some will give you a full refund while others will just bus you to the next location. These are just some of the things to consider when looking into this mode of travel.

CRUISE SHIP:

Allows going to areas that would be expensive to fly to. Another great advantage is that you pack and unpack only once and experience new places at every port. For myself personally, I have found that this offers the best value for my travel choice.

As is true with all forms of travel, there are some drawbacks to consider. The first is that you are limited to where the cruise line goes to. There are usually additional costs for the tours, gratuities are extra, drinks are expensive, and added cost for using wifi needs to be looked at when determining whether this is the best value for you. Cruising is a leisure way of traveling for seniors. If this mode of travel is something you are considering and want to get the best value, then I would recommend that you stick with one cruise line. The advantages of being loyal are definitely rewarded. Once you reach a certain level with the cruise line, preferred boarding, special cocktail parties, and other amenities are there for you and your guests.

MYTHS OF CRUISING

I realize that oftentimes there are myths surrounding cruising. I would like to address some of these at this time.

Myth 1: Cruises are crowded.

It is amazing how 4000 people can be on a ship, and it will not feel crowded. The way the new ships are designed with so many places for people to congregate, the feeling of crowds really is a myth.

Myth 2: Cruises are for old people.

That is only true on certain cruise lines.

Holland America typically caters to an over 65 age group, but the other cruise lines do not.

Carnival typically targets young people and young families.

RCL and NCL both target multi-generations.

Myth 3: I'll get seasick.

There are options for patches and pills that can help. Also booking a room mid-ship helps the movement. An inside room is a good choice as you will not be seeing the movement of the water from your room.

Myth 4: I'll get noro-virus.

The cruise lines are well aware of diseases and have hand sanitizers at every place that people congregate. It also has signage to remind people to wash their hands frequently. A cruise ship is no worse than going to a mall in your neighborhood for the potential of catching a germ. The rules are the same – wash your hands thoroughly and often.

Myth 5: Everybody's drunk.

The costs of drinks are not cheap. Most drink packages limit how much alcohol can be consumed on any given day. The drinking age limit for someone wanting to cruise is 21. Carnival cruise line, which tags themselves as "The Fun Ship," tends to attract a younger crowd which you may find has a tendency to party more.

Myth 6: I'll be bored.

Only if you choose to will you be bored. Every day the cruise ship lists all the extra activities they have available besides the normal activities onboard. While in port, numerous excursions are available for your various interests.

Myth 7: Cruises are dangerous.

Not sure where this comes from as driving your car is more dangerous. The odds are very low against something happening on a cruise ship.

Myth 8: A cruise isn't a cultural experience.

It is amazing how many wonderful people you will meet at the various activities. Choosing share a table at meals opens opportunities to meet people from all over the world. Also each port you visit is a world in and of itself.

Myth 9: There will be too many kids

This is only on certain ships that cater to families. Princess Cruises, Holland America, Celebrity and luxury cruises usually don't have large amounts of children on their cruises as their clientele are older or wealthier.

Myth 10: I have to eat with people I don't know.

There are 3 dining options, early, late and open dining. If you do not want to sit with people you don't know, than all you have to do is opt for a seat for one (or two) at any of the dining options.

Myth 11: I'll be too busy.

This again is a choice you make. Activities abound, but you get to choose how many you want to participate in. If you want to just sit on your balcony or around the pool and enjoy a good book, that is your choice.

Myth 12: I have to get dressed up.

Depending on the length of the cruise, they may have one or more formal nights for the dining rooms. If you chose not to eat in the dining room, then no formal attire is required for your entire trip. Again it's all about choices that you get to make.

Myth 13: I can't cruise alone.

More and more singles are cruising, and the cruise lines are now making adjustments to accommodate singles. Single rooms on their newer ships are being offered, and meet and greet opportunities for people traveling solo are being made available.

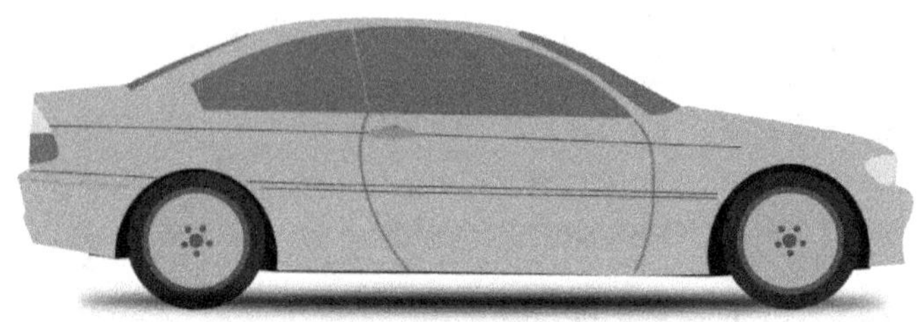

TRAVELING

BY

CAR

- ❖ Plan to make frequent stops. My husband and I stop every 2 hours to stretch and switch drivers. Use the stop times that works best for you.
- ❖ Prior to your trip, map out points of interest, and if possible, build those attractions into your stop-and-stretch schedule.
- ❖ If visiting museums or parks, invest in the lifetime senior pass for $80 that allows you free entrance to all national parks in the USA. There is also an annual senior pass for $20.
- ❖ Never pass up an opportunity to use a bathroom (never know where the next one is).
- ❖ Keep your canes and walkers easily accessible.
- ❖ Keep medications handy.
- ❖ When traveling to a new area, make sure that you have enough gas. You never know where the next gas station is.

HOW TO FIND THE BEST ROAD STOPS:

- ❖ Identify the official rest areas before you leave on your trip. Most states list their welcome centers and rest areas online.

❖ Do your research on roadside businesses. If you have a Smartphone, doing a quick search on Yelp or Trip Advisor before your stop will help you choose between several gas stations.

❖ Time your stops if you can.

❖ Planning your road trip can help you avoid not finding any stops for gas, food, bathrooms, and lodging.

HOW TO BOOK A HOTEL THE SMART WAY:

❖ Start with a thorough search. Check an online travel agency like Expedia or Booking.com or call your travel agent. Check the rate against the price your preferred hotel would charge if you book direct.

❖ Review the restrictions. Hotels can impose restrictions for booking through their site, like making their rooms non-refundable. Read the conditions closely before deciding where to book. You might be better off working with a big agency that has negotiated better terms.

❖ Check the incentives offered by the hotel. Ask yourself what is more important – cost, points or upgrades.

HOW TO FIGHT QUESTIONABLE CAR RENTAL TACTICS:

❖ Sign up for a company's frequent-renter program, which allows you to state your preferences before you arrive. That could make you less vulnerable to upgrade, downgrade and option games.

❖ Automated check-in kiosks limit the amount of interaction with a salesperson. But pay close attention to what you're agreeing to on the screen.

TIPS FOR GETTING A VEHICLE WHEN THEY RUN OUT OF RENTAL CARS:

❖ Confirm your reservation: Contact your car rental agency a day before you arrive. Always bring your reservation confirmation with you to show the rate you booked. Make a printout, just in case the battery on your phone dies.

❖ Arrive on time: Check in as close as possible to the time indicated on your reservation.

❖ Have a Plan B: That could mean renting from a competitor, taking a bus or using a cab or a popular ride-sharing service.

HOW TO AVOID FEES ON YOUR RENTAL CAR:

❖ Tolls: Find out where they are. GPS may show you another route. If you choose to do a toll road, realize that any tolls will be charged to your credit card at a later date?

❖ Do you buy the rental company's car insurance? Car rental insurance is oftentimes offered as an added feature on your credit card, travel insurance policy, or your own personal car insurance. It can also be a standalone product offered by your online travel agency. Check into this before you head to the car rental place.

❖ Tickets – tough one, as there are times when you are not aware what the speed is and being in a strange place doesn't help, yet it is not an excuse for not knowing according to the police. You can download an app like Speed Cameras & Traffic by Sygic, which lets you see the speed limit for the road you are traveling on, or CamSam Plus which alerts you to speed cameras. Many GPS navigation systems also display posted speed limits and traffic enforcement warnings.

ITEMS FOR CAR TRAVEL:

- ❖ Extra Antifreeze
- ❖ Jumper cables
- ❖ Extra Motor oil
- ❖ Windshield wiper fluid
- ❖ Maps and driving directions
- ❖ Spare keys
- ❖ Pillows and blankets
- ❖ Ice scraper
- ❖ Small container for change for parking meters and toll roads
- ❖ Spare tire and tire iron
- ❖ Water
- ❖ Snacks

IF DRIVING YOUR OWN CAR:

Before setting out, check your tire pressures (don't forget to check your spare tire), oil, transmission, and brake fluid levels, windshield washer fluid level, and antifreeze level.

MULTI

GENERATIONAL

TRAVEL

QUESTIONS TO ASK:

- ❖ Who will be traveling?
- ❖ Who will be paying for the trip?
- ❖ What are the places that everyone wants to see?
- ❖ What are the places that specific groups want to see?
- ❖ What are the ages of everyone traveling?
- ❖ Are there health or physical challenges for anyone in the group?
- ❖ Is anyone celebrating a significant event? Birthday? Anniversary?
- ❖ Will places visited be of significance to your past history?
- ❖ Who will be the decision makers for activities and destinations?
- ❖ Will it be a group decision or will the person paying make all the decisions?
- ❖ What about the accommodations - will there be need for large suites or vacation rentals?
- ❖ Who will arrange for activities?
- ❖ Will there be activities scheduled for everyone?

Be realistic in your expectations as to what you want to see happen on this trip.

Arrange times to rest and relax – trying to cram too many activities in will only wear everyone out.

Realize that different age groups (young children and seniors) have different energy levels – make sure you address each in activities and rest times.

Norwegian Cruise line is the best for multi-age groups.

Check locations to see if they have activities for all age levels traveling.

Some packed items can be shared by multiple users.

Make sure that you talk about what is working and what needs to change even while you are traveling.

If taking a tour, make sure that the tour is appropriate for all ages traveling.

Make sure you purchase travel insurance for everyone traveling. One person getting sick or hurt before the trip can affect everyone's finances if the trip has to be cancelled.

Take lots of pictures of all the fun times and memories shared.

Make sure everyone is on WhatsApp to communicate with one another during the trip

FAMILY CRUISES:

These specific cruise ships are geared for multigenerational families. They have something for everyone of all ages. They include excursions that are geared for families.

Note it is the cruise ship not the cruise line. So going on a Coral Princess is not the same experience as the Regal Princess, same cruise line but definitely a different atmosphere. When booking a cruise, you need to make sure you know what ship you will be on if you want the family experience.

SAFARI ENDEAVOUR – is a small ship with amazing opportunities for exotic experiences. Only 84 passengers so the price is on the high side.

NORWEGIAN GETAWAY - Sports a 5 waterslide park, miniature bowling alley, rock climbing, and bungee trampoline just to mention a few. They really want to capture the multi-generational market. Every new ship built by the cruise line is bigger and better than the last.

DISNEY FANTASY – is and always will be for families of all ages – no discounts and very pricey but worth the experience.

ROYAL CARIBBEAN ANTHEM OF THE SEAS -
It is a ship for families, with bumper cars and skydiving experiences, along with good things for the adults.

CARNIVAL FREEDOM - Carnival is noted for the fun ship. Most of its clientele are young families and singles – drinking and partying seems to be its theme.

REGAL PRINCESS - Princess has one of the most loyal following of all cruise ship lines and its target market is the 45 to 65 year olds. The Regal is designed for families.

MSC DIVINA – offers Aqua Cycling, Formula race car simulators. They are trying to hedge into the family market.

HOLLAND AMERICA NIEUW AMSTERDAM -
They have few activities for kids (note most of the other Holland America's clientele are the over 65 age group).

CUNARD'S QUEEN ELIZABETH – family ship is formal and elegant. Activities include: playing crochet, chess, air hockey and crafts. It is very low key.

CELEBRITY REFLECTION – is an upscale ship that is really targeting millennials – some activities for younger children are available. For children who can't take a lot of stimulus, this would be a good choice.

ACTIVITIES:

All activites and tours will indicate the activity level. These are categorized from easy walking to lots of stairs and uneven terrain. It can also include the various lengths of each trek of the tour. Pay attention to this because being out of shape and having to hike or walk for long lenghts of time when you are not used to it, can put a damper on your fun to enjoy the activity or sight.

Make sure you schedule down time after each activity.

Try to incorporate something that everyone wants when traveling in a group.

Allow for individuals to go on their own or with other groups when traveling.

SPECIAL NEEDS TRAVEL

SPECIAL NEEDS TRAVEL

❖ Make arrangements for any special needs, including mobility requirements, dietary selections and other services that will be needed while traveling before you go.

❖ Make sure there are ADA compliant rooms.

❖ Contact airlines, hotels, cruise or tour to let them know of any challenges you may have. Ask what they have to offer that might assist in each of your concerned areas.

❖ Get them to confirm in writing what is being offered.

❖ In some cases special forms and a doctor's verification are required.

❖ **Specialglobe.com** helps families planning trips with special needs.

❖ There are special airport programs that help autistic children.

❖ What challenges will need to be addressed - wheel chair ramps, dietary needs, etc.?

❖ Work with special agents or companies trained specifically for special needs travel.

❖ Plan ahead and play the "what if" game, creating different scenarios of what could happen, then work out possible solutions for each.

❖ Be flexible.

❖ Research where you want to go while ranking the places as to what they have for people with special needs.

❖ Plan how you will get around.

❖ Prepare for air travel.

❖ Plan hotels wisely.

❖ Choose carefully the right destination.

❖ Hire a pro.

BLIND OR LOW VISION – Traveling Abroad

Disclose your disability to request accommodations well in advance. If blind or low vision, there are organizations you can contact for the region you wish to visit.

Arrange a time for orientation training – so that you can get to know the immediate area and surroundings.

Research public transportation - buses and trains
How reliable are they?
What services do they provide for people with disabilities?

Be prepared for different attitudes on disability.
In some countries people with disabilities are rarely seen in public. Don't be distressed at cultural differences.

Contact airports and airlines ahead of time
Request "meet and assist" at any airport you will visit. Make sure the flight attendants know your disability.

Research required documentation and vaccinations for service animals.

Consider Traveling with an assistant.

WHAT TO BRING:

- ❖ Take a cane.
- ❖ Take a laptop with a screen reader or other assistive technology.

TIPS ONCE YOU ARE ABROAD:

❖ **Ask Questions.**

❖ **Be prepared to educate strangers** about effective guidance techniques – let people know what you prefer.

❖ **Connect with locals** who are blind or low vision in the area.

❖ **Learn the currency.**

❖ **Learn how the toilets work** and if you have to pay for them.

❖ **Carry written directions** for important locations.

❖ **Crossing streets:** If rules of the road are not known, cross with the locals.

❖ **Find a taxi driver you trust or hire a limo service.** Arrange for them to pick you up and take you around.

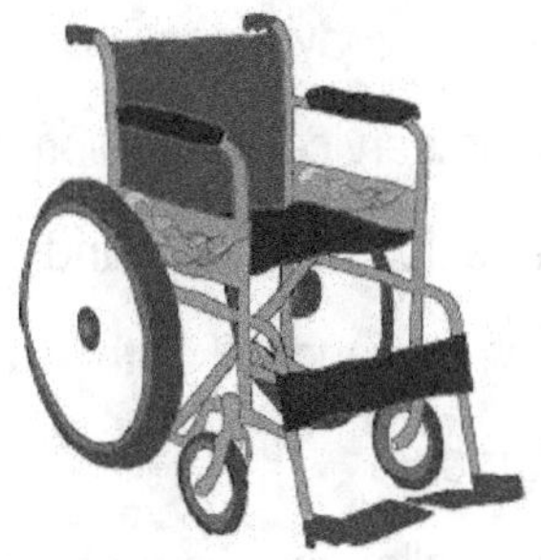

Issues that have to be addressed:

Wheel chairs, scooters, canes, walkers, crutches, and prosthetics - how will you get around?

Are the areas you are visiting something you can navigate?

If not what alternatives do they have available?

Wheel chair – manual or battery operated? What resources are available to recharge your battery?

Does the wheelchair fold up and can it be stored in a bus or car? Is the tour bus equipped to handle wheel chairs?

If you use a walker, can you get on and off the bus (ship or train)?

Do you have to rent these mobility devices at your destination, or do you have to bring your own?

Know the size of your chair as it will be important in determining where it can be stored or accessed.

What about other items you may need in a foreign country? Where can you find services or equipment?

Tender boats on cruise ships cannot handle wheel chairs or scooters. Getting on and off with a cane or walker also could be hazardous.

River boats can also be a challenge – some cruise lines are trying to make accommodations so check before you book.

Challenges with speech – traveling with a companion that can aid is an asset or the trip might be very frustrating for you and for those who you are trying to communicate with.

Service animals – do they allow them in an area – what kinds of restrictions and limitations are in place?

What about requiring help getting up out of a chair? Bathing? Toileting? Transferring? Do you need assistance?

Oxygen/Ventilator? What do you need to bring? Where will you find a replacement if something malfunctions or is lost?

BOTTOM LINE: MAKE SURE THAT YOU ASK QUESTIONS & GET RESPONSES IN WRITING.

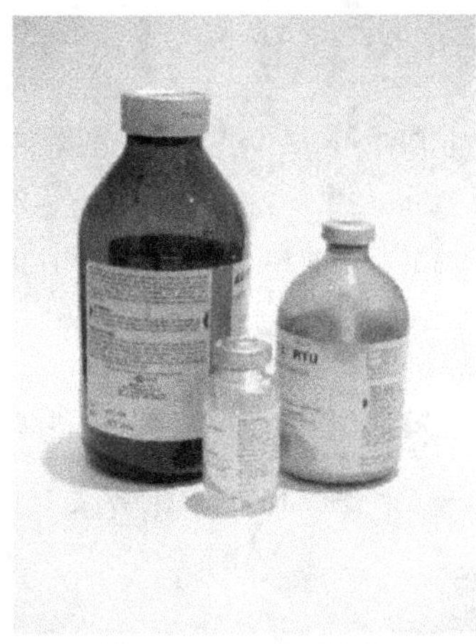

MEDICATION

❖ Consult your doctor before planning a trip.

❖ Check to see if there are any vaccines needed.

❖ Make sure you have enough medication to cover twice your needs for the time you are on the trip.

❖ Carry your meds in your carryon with you on the plane.

❖ Have a copy of all meds being taken along with instructions for their use. Store them separately from meds.

❖ When traveling in different time zones, set an alarm when a medication needs to be taken.

❖ Keep all prescriptions and over-the-counter medications in the same bag and in original containers.

HOW TO AVOID SMELLS AT HOTELS:

This is a serious issue for individuals with disabilities involving smells. We live in polluted environments, our air is often sprayed to death with perfumes that oftentimes are an irritant to many individuals.

- ❖ Look into hotels that offer hypoallergenic rooms. Most of the major chains now offer these types of rooms.

- ❖ If you detect an unusual odor, do not unpack but call the front desk and request a different room immediately. If the front desk doesn't address the issue, then request speaking to the manager.

- ❖ Bring a scented spray that you can use on your linens. My favorite is lavender which also helps me sleep when I am in a strange place.

A GREAT TRIP DOES NOT HAVE TO BE A NIGHTMARE OF CHALLENGES.

CONSIDER EACH STEP OF THE TRIP INDIVIDUALLY AND FIND OUT WHAT IS INVOLVED IN ADDRESSING YOUR PERSONAL LIMITATIONS. GET THE FACTS.

Dietary Restrictions

Legal Disclaimer:

Please note that we are not licensed medical professionals. We do not diagnose, treat, or prescribe for any illness or health issue. The information or advice provided here should not be construed as medical advice. If you chose to use any of the natural remedies or advice discussed here, you will be taking responsibility for your own health and wellness. The statements and information on this website have not been evaluated by the U.S. Food and Drug Administration

Hi

There,

I am Ian

Sandage

I am a Nutritional Therapy & Restorative Wellness Practitioner (NTP/RWP), blogger, animal lover and husband on a personal mission to be the change that I want to see in this world.

I am also a certified personal trainer & health coach through The American Council on Exercise (ACE) as well as a sports nutrition specialist.

On a completely different level, I am also a certified customer support manager with a degree in Network Technology that has been my other line of work for the last twenty years.

In my spare time I love to pick up the guitar and create music. I enjoy being in the kitchen to cook creative whole food nutritious meals. I am always seeking to replicate old favorite dishes with better whole food ingredients. I am in love with the mountains and feel truly blessed to have chosen beautiful Colorado Springs as our new home! We believe in giving animals a good home and have taken in many over the years! My wife and I spend a lot of our time enjoying the outdoors on hikes and exploring our new Colorado passion! And lastly, I love to learn anything new whether it be a new song on the guitar or listening to a new audio book; it all has great value to me.

I learned I had Ulcerative Colitis in 2003. After being diagnosed with this, I experienced many years of ups and downs. In 2015 I had an epic flare that would not stop, and it was at this crossroads that I decided to take a different path on this health journey. I cleaned up my diet and environment and ultimately restored my digestive balance to a point where the flares stopped and real healing actually began. This journey has been so ultra-rewarding for me to not only learn about how to be in harmony with my body, but also to be able to guide others through the same maze and out the other side to good health. I have essentially become a student of my own life and want to help others to do the same!

Through this process, I learned about the number of foods that I had become sensitive to which significantly altered how I co-existed in my environment. I had to learn on the fly how to fit into a country that was so massively focused on convenience that when I sat down and actually thought about the prospect of traveling, it created a huge amount of stress for me. Like many others in this situation, I resisted doing it because I felt that it was just going to be too hard. But what I can say is that I found methods that worked for me, and ultimately the confidence that I gained by doing this helped to propel me to even greater health achievements in all facets of my own health recovery.

We strive to make things easier in this country which comes at a pretty hefty price as far as our health is concerned, and anytime we travel out we are pressed with getting here to there with little thought about the things in between.

We disregard any food planning because the infrastructure is setup to cater to the majority to provide quick energy. If you have five dollars, you can get a burger, fries and drink in less than five minutes and be on your way. So what if this meal is comprised of everything you were just told that you are sensitive to and need to abstain from it? What if what you eat will ultimately make or break how much enjoyment you can have on that trip? What are you to do? The last thing you want to do is to try to rough it and go the entire day in the airport terminal without eating; it's a recipe for disaster. There is a very simple guide that will help you to design a travel plan that will allow you to move from home to your destination with minimal discomfort.

Before I started on this journey in 2015, I ate what I wanted without any thought of what was in my food, and quite honestly I never gave much thought to those who were dealing with food issues. I feel a great deal of empathy these days for others who have to restrict what they eat. I have learned a lot about myself and how to do those things that I once thought were nearly impossible.

The number one thing to remember is that attitude is everything. While it is difficult to travel with these special needs, regardless of how you travel, it is very doable to maintain your lifestyle and stay in alignment with the things you personally need to do to keep healthy. What this requires first and foremost is the right attitude and expectations about it all. Be willing to go easy on yourself. The bottom line is that the food & travel industries are not really setup to cater to people with special needs. We are seeing more food options for those with sensitivities, but it's not nearly enough to be able to rely on there being options while away from home.

The second thing that is critical to your success is that you really have to put on a detective cap and understand what is in the food that you are consuming. This is where you have to get good at doing research. Learn to understand ingredients very well and what's in your food. Pull out Google and start looking at what you can eat without issue that's available at the airport, on the ship or along the road. You need to be careful here though and ask the right questions to understand more about what's in the food, how it is cooked, gluten free surfaces & cooking utensils used, cooking oils, other ingredients, fillers, additives, preservatives and so on. MSG is a big one that I see a lot of clients have issue with, and it's in a lot of processed food out there. So let's get to the things you can do that you may not have thought of. These are not exhaustive lists, but rather things that I have found have personally worked for me.

LET'S START WITH AIRPLANE AND AIRPORT TRAVEL FIRST.

Always plan ahead. Planning is essential to avoid being stranded in a terminal due to flight delays or whatever it may be without something you can eat.

Give yourself extra time when booking. Stress and poor time management will lead to choices that will ultimately derail your efforts.

Study the layout of the airport and where any gluten free/special needs food may be located in proximity to your gate.

Most major airports have at least two gluten free options to select from, but you will want to identify where these are located to make sure you have time. Email **nfo@gffmag.com** to check on gluten free airport options. Establishments that offer gluten free options are typically more aware of the people who have special foods needs, and quite often you can work with the staff to alert them of your special requirements.

Speak with a manager if you have additional concerns, or call these places ahead of time to ask questions.

Look at menus carefully. Establishments that offer special needs foods are very clear on their menus about how the food is prepared, while in other cases there will be almost zero mention of how the food is prepared.

If you cannot locate an option, try to stick with places that you can order just meat and or vegetables. Always ask for no seasoning, sauces or anything that could have food sensitive ingredients, and skip the breads as well as grain-based products. These typically are the worst offending items that you could consume, and be aware of condiments especially.

Carry an empty, reusable non-plastic bottle for water once you get into the terminal areas. You can purchase a travel filter like the Life Straw Personal Water Filter that will allow you to filter & drink on the go. Water quality is an important piece to your health. It's not just about food that can cause stress in the body.

If you have very limited options even outside of just gluten free, you will want to do some extra planning and preparation. A lot of people are not aware that you can freeze liquids and bring them through security. Just make sure to alert the screener of special food in your carryon that is frozen.

SOME GREAT NUTRIENT DENSE OPTIONS:

Pack an unrefined sea salt. An unprocessed sea salt will have a full complement of minerals that when used in your water will serve as an electrolyte. Just put a pinch in each glass of water you are drinking to reap the benefits.

Avocados are a super food and are just loaded with nutrients. Pound per pound you will be hard-pressed to find another food that is this complete.

Hard boiled eggs are easy to eat, and what we are going for is a food that packs a lot of nutrients in a small package. Eggs fit this profile.

Homemade breads - I love to make breads, and you can add a little honey when you make it so that it's like a snack. This is a perfect comfort road food.

Freeze some fresh-made bone broth and carry on frozen. You can run your container under hot water in the bathroom to liquefy it, and get hot water in a cup to drink it with. Bone broth is loaded with proteins and amino acids and is very satisfying.

Grass-fed butter or ghee is a great way to get some good fats on the run.

Coconut butter & oil (frozen) will help to keep you satiated, plus it has anti-microbial benefits which can be helpful on the road.

NUTS & SEEDS

Chia seeds specifically will help you stay hydrated longer. Just sprinkle on food or in your beverages.

Hemp seeds are another great super food option. Loonutrition profile of this seed and it's pretty complete.

Any non-liquid fruits & vegetables

Grass fed protein powders/bars

I like to take things along that lift the spirits. Take your favorite spices along. I am a huge turmeric & ginger fan. They go well with a lot of foods, plus they are loaded with health benefits. Or how about a piece of organic dark chocolate?

Skip dehydrated foods like jerky and dried fruits as you want to consume more foods with higher water content to stay hydrated. We don't drink enough water as it is typically, but traveling amplifies this greatly, and dehydrated foods will not help you stay hydrated.

Check out the following for more items
you can bring through security :

https://www.tsa.gov/travel/security-screening/whatcanibring/food

In a crunch, you can make soups/stews. Heat them before you leave for the airport, put them in an insulated thermos, and consume before going through security. The thermos must be empty prior to going through security, but this could give you an opportunity to sit down for a few and have a home cooked meal before you embark.

HOW ABOUT WHEN YOU NEED TO STAY IN A HOTEL?

I always look for a hotel that has a full kitchen including stovetop, pans and full refrigerator. My personal favorite is the Staybridge Suites, and it is not any more expensive than other hotel chains that don't have full kitchen setups. Many times these places are actually less expensive than other non-full kitchen rooms, so I think it's a no-brainer to go with a full kitchen setup.

Locate grocery options nearby. I always try to find a Natural Grocers or a local whole foods type grocery store nearby to not only eat the way I want to eat, but to save money while away from home. Eating out takes a toll on your wallet as well as your health.

Get filtered water from the same Whole Foods, Natural Grocers or other locations that have reverse osmosis filtered water. You can purchase jugs by the gallon and can return them to get your refund back when finished.

Some hotels will allow personal hot plates, induction cookers, crock-pots and other cookers which can be great options. Just make sure to check if you are allowed to use these devices in the room. If you happen to be driving to your location, then this is a doable option, but may be limited to a small hot plate/pan in your checked bags if flying.

I am not a fan of the microwave, but in a pinch you can get creative and make daily meals in the microwave if need be. Start with whole fresh foods and a microwave safe dish, and you can still eat fairly well in a kitchen without a stove. Skip the microwaveable meals as they are just loaded with junk typically. You can get some organic options, but you are not really in control of what's in the food. The goal is to control the ingredients.

Driving to your location?

It is a little easier to find good whole food choices while road traveling. Take a look at your route and do some research. Check out:

https://www.findmeglutenfree.com/ to find local options for your location.

If you are restricted beyond gluten, or if your route is more rural, it becomes important to pack what you need.

Use a Styrofoam cooler or cool/heat insulated bag to keep perishables safe. I order a lot of meat and get coolers that I repurpose for alternative uses including using them for traveling.

Using an insulated thermos, I will make bone broth and a nice meat/veggie stew to travel with. A good thermos will keep your food hot for a good eight hours, and I always plan to have two meals in the car.

Pack silverware, utensils, paper towels and trash bags.

Don't forget to bring vitamin supplements. I always travel with a few key things like HCL, probiotics, multi vitamins, Vitamin C and digestive enzymes.

Easy snacks like banana bread, guacamole, hard boiled eggs, or nuts and seeds are great choices. I will make fat bombs (coconut oil, nuts, grass fed collagen powder, cacao powder, honey) and freeze these for the trip. Skip the convenience store junk food and load up on good fats.

Crock-pot & Instant Pots are great cooking devices to take along for use at your final destination.

Filtered jugs of water – I bring a gallon jug at least of filtered water.

Traveling on the water?

It may be easier to find what you are looking for on a cruise ship, but nonetheless stay vigilant as there are still many opportunities for things to go in an adverse direction.

Call the cruise line well in advance about your needs. You may want to arrange some visits of the cooking areas to establish a relationship with the staff who will be preparing the food.

Get to know your chefs and managers by making contact the first day on board. Cruise lines love to take care of their passengers, and you can ask for what you need.

If you find a restaurant that seems to fit your needs, don't be afraid to stick with it. Be careful with new staff and new places as there are thousands of passengers, and they cannot be expected to remember everyone.

Work with the staff to help identify suitable on-shore locations to eat at, and ask if they will help to contact these spots to alert them of your special needs.

It may be best to skip the buffet lines unless you know for certain what is in the food you are consuming.

Keep a copy of your dietary needs with you for reference.

Don't assume anything. Ask questions and don't be afraid to confirm things multiple times throughout your trip. There are a lot of ingredients that may seem simple to others, but will wreak havoc with those with sensitivities.

Worst case scenario planning dictates that you bring along some items from home that you can consume just in case. Focus on non-perishable foods referenced throughout this guide like avocados, protein bars/powders, good fats, etc.

GENERAL TIP

The same principles of good planning apply to all forms of travel. Call ahead and ask questions. See if you can make arrangements wherever you are headed to that will accommodate your needs.

It takes practice to be willing to engage people on these things, and a lot of times we feel like we are being a nuisance to others by asking so many questions and requests. But this is a very key thing that one has to get good with if they want to be able to co-exist in this convenience food filled country.

As mentioned earlier, take digestive enzymes along with you. In a crunch, this will help you to digest those things that you may have a problem with. Just find a reputable brand and do some research on quality products that contain a broad spectrum of enzymes that help support digestion of fats, carbohydrates and proteins.

Bentonite Clay is another useful supplement to have along with you if you have food sensitivities. If you have consumed something that interacts with you adversely, try this to help mitigate the reactions as soon as possible. Drink plenty of water with it and look for organic options.

I never leave home without a good quality probiotic. To keep things in balance, find a good quality supplement to take daily. It's especially important to take while traveling as we tend to get out of balance either one way or another.

PLAN AHEAD FOR 3-5 DAYS PRIOR TO YOUR TRIP

Stay hydrated. Drink 1/2 your body weight in ounces. So if you weigh 150 pounds, drink 75 ounces of clean water daily. Account for diuretics like coffee, sodas, tea, etc. by consuming an extra 10-16 ounces for every 8 ounces of diuretic consumed. This is one of the best things you can do to achieve success.

You may want to look at doubling up your probiotics days ahead of your trip. This will help to ready your body for changes in your environment and crowd out the bad guys.

Vitamin "S" for sleep. Get good quality 8-10 hours prior to your trip.

Don't assume anything. Food sensitivities are just not always on everyone's radar. There are misconceptions about just how sensitive you may be to cross contamination, obscure ingredients, etc. Always ask questions and do your research.

I hope this guide helps you to have a more enjoyable trip wherever it takes you. For myself, I learned a lot by trial and error, and ultimately I have found ways to make this all flow much nicer. You can do this also if you just remember to stop and breathe and plan well. Don't be afraid to ask questions or what someone might think of your efforts to stay healthy. This is your life, and you have to do the things you need to do for yourself.

For additional questions about this section or to inquire about how you can work with us regarding food sensitivities or any other health aspect, please check out the following:

https://www.hearttohealthwellness.com/

hearttohealthwellness@gmail.com

https://www.instagram.com/hearttohealthwellness/

TAKING

A

TOUR

TAKING A TOUR

If you're planning on taking a group tour:

- ❖ Be realistic about your itinerary.
- ❖ Which travel companies are friendly to seniors: Holland America, Princes or Oceania for cruising
- ❖ Tour Groups: Collette, Monograms, Brendan, CIE
- ❖ River Cruises: Avalon, AmaWaterways, Amadeus and Uniworld
- ❖ Consider renting a chauffeured car for a couple of hours to tour highlights of a town.

TOURS, HOTELS, CRUISES AND TRAINS

- ❖ Contact the companies you will be traveling with for any special requests.
- ❖ Don't forget to inform anyone you will be staying with if you are celebrating any special event (birthday, anniversary).

TRAVEL ADVISOR

To Use or Not To Use?

Is It A Good Idea?

TRAVEL ADVISOR – TO USE OR NOT TO USE
(Why is it a good idea?)

- ❖ It doesn't cost you any more for their services (unless they choose to add an extra fee, but in that case, they should tell you that they are doing that).
- ❖ You have someone who will be your go-to person for every aspect of your trip.
- ❖ Your contact person if you need to make changes or something unexpected comes up.
- ❖ Sign you up with **WhatsApp** when you are traveling in a foreign country so that there is no charge for calling them.
- ❖ Will handle all details from the moment you decide where you want to go and when.
- ❖ Will find you the best deals and prices.
- ❖ Will make all the arrangements with the hotel, airline, and tours if traveling with any challenges.
- ❖ Realize that travel companies want to please the travel advisor more than you because they are a source of repeat business whereas you are a one-time deal for the most part.

TAKING CARE

OF

BASICS

SAFETY CONCERNS

- ❖ Consider using a money belt or fanny pack that goes under clothing.
- ❖ If a purse is needed, carry a crossover one where you have it sit in the front of you – make sure that the strap is leather and rather large.
- ❖ Most places accept credit cards – notify your credit company that you will be traveling and to which countries you will be visiting.
- ❖ Inquire about daily limits on your card – each credit card company has a daily specific limit.
- ❖ Make a copy of the credit card you are carrying.
- ❖ Don't bring debit cards – no insurance will cover them if they are stolen.
- ❖ Visa still is the best card.
- ❖ Notify your cell phone company of your travels.
- ❖ Find out about any special international plans for your phone if traveling in foreign countries.

HOW TO PREVENT YOUR IDENTITY FROM BEING STOLEN:

Don't play fast and loose with your ID. Your passport and ID are some of the most important travel documents. Don't leave them in your hotel room unless you lock them in a room safe. And when you carry them on your person, keep them close to you, preferably in a money belt or travel wallet.

Keep 'em separated. Don't store all critical documents in the same place. You may need one in order to replace the other.

Upload scanned copies of critical documents online. A copy of a document by itself will not allow you to travel, but it can make the process to replace a passport a whole lot easier.

RESERVATIONS:

Call to confirm before your visit. Yes, even if you booked directly with the hotel or rental car.

Double check your dates.

What I do for clients is actually do a spreadsheet with a time line of every moving part of the vacation.

When I have done the spreadsheet, this allows me to find gaps in the trip schedule, especially dates that are not matching to what I thought I had scheduled. This is also a good time to contact each location or vendor to see if they have the same information that you have. People make mistakes – don't allow your vacation to be ruined by oversight either by you or the places you plan to visit.

Double checking the facts assures that you have the name, phone number and reservation number of each item of your vacation. Make a printout of your reservation. A hard copy printout remains the most reliable evidence of your reservation. Taking a picture of it on your phone is also another option.

HOW TO KEEP YOUR TRAVEL COMPLAINT FROM BEING IGNORED:

Find out who is in charge, talk to them, don't waste time talking with people who don't have the authority to make any decisions.

If you are staying at a hotel and there are issues, contact the manager of the facility. Explain what the problem is and indicate how you feel they can fix it for you.

I recently had a client who went to a very upscale hotel in Maui only to find out that the hotel was doing serious construction outside her window from 6:30 am in the morning until 7 pm in the evening. Now on their website they did mention that they were doing construction, but they also felt it would not be an issue to anyone booking with them. Obviously that was not the case.

The client complained. I got involved as she was my client, and the hotel management was able to place her in an upgraded room on the other side of the hotel away from where the main construction was happening.

She was also given a credit on her bill and a voucher for a free breakfast at the buffet for the inconvenience this caused her.

Some basic rules:

BE NICE BUT BE FIRM.

If they are unwilling to budge, then post on **TRIP ADVISOR**. No one wants a bad review. In many cases, this will prompt the customer service representative for the company to address your concerns.

If they are a corporate chain, write a complaint letter to the main office – customer service department. By writing, I have been able to receive free night stays and other amenities when there was a glitch that they should have handled on site.

TRAVEL INSURANCE

* ❖ Unless you can predict your future – I would strongly suggest buying a basic policy to give you peace of mind.

* ❖ There are several different ways you can purchase travel insurance. One is to purchase through the individual companies that are handling each individual part of your trip. Read the policy as some will give you 100% back while others will give you credit on a future trip. They also will only cover the parts of the trip that they are handling.

* ❖ Another way is to buy an independent policy, say with Travel Guard, that covers the cost of the entire trip. This is very important if you have multiple vendors you are dealing with. An independent policy, in most cases, also gives you life insurance, accident insurance, and medical benefits.

WHO TO CALL IF YOUR TRAVEL INSURANCE CLAIM HAS BEEN DENIED:

Check why it was denied – If the reason is because you did not buy a policy that covers that item, there is basically nothing you can do.

On the other hand, if you feel that what happened was covered under the terms of your coverage, than maybe it would warrant a letter to your insurance commissioner with a copy to the travel insurance company. To find your insurance commissioner, visit the National Association of Insurance Commissioners site: naic.org/index_members.htm. There have been times that travelers have reported that their claims were honored after copying their state insurance commissioner on their appeal.

WHAT STANDARD TRAVEL INSURANCE DOESN'T COVER?

Pre-existing medical conditions – I had a situation where the client had cancer several years before and wanted to go on a cruise. When she started having complications with walking because she needed a hip replacement, she had to cancel her trip because the doctor wanted to schedule her surgery. As they were doing the tests for the surgery, they discovered that the cancer had come back. In this case, the travel insurance did pay her even though the cancer came back. The reason they paid was that the original cancellation was based on her needing hip surgery, a new medical condition. Usually the pre-existing exclusion is 6 to 12 months prior to booking the insurance.

If you changed your mind and do not take the vacation, that is not covered unless you bought a cancel-for-any-reason policy.

Cancellations due to circumstances under your control but not the fault of a specific vendor may not be covered. For example, if you got to the airport late because you did not give yourself sufficient time and you missed your flight. If you can prove that not getting to the airport on time was out of your control, then you have a case for getting refunded for your trip. For example, if you had left to get to the airport in plenty of time but an accident or some other act, which was out of your control, dictated your late arrival at the airport.

HOW TO AVOID A VACATION RENTAL SURPRISE:

Apply some common sense rules."

Rent with names you found on trusted websites: Airbnb, VRBO and FlipKey all have legitimate websites where they list rentals.

Ask what comes with the rentals.

Get a detailed list of everything that will be provided. Never assume – just ask.

If you verified the legitimacy of the rental, confirm with a credit card. If possible use PayPal when making a payment. In no event should you wire them money.

Remember you may find a cheaper location, but you run the risk of it not being what it claims to be, and in the end, it could cost you a lot more money and inconvenience and stress. Even getting references does not guarantee that the place is legit. Some places will have their friends, who are in on the scam, be the ones posting on how great the place is. The old adage "Buyer beware" is still good common sense.

TRAVEL DOCUMENTS

* ❖ Make (2) copies of your passport - keep them in separate locations – one in your carry-on and another in your checked bag.

* ❖ Email a copy of your passport to your travel agent.

* ❖ Give your emergency contact person your travel schedule.

* ❖ Give emergency contact information to your travel agent.

* ❖ If visiting someone send them your flight schedule.

* ❖ Have copies of your travel insurance, Visas, emergency contacts and medical information with you.

❖ Know What to Expect on Your Trip- make sure your travel agent gives you a detailed outline of every aspect of your trip with all pertinent information along with phone numbers of everyone involved in your trip.

❖ Know what your limits for bringing in items for custom and immigration forms (don't be afraid to ask the flight attendant for help)

❖ Make sure you understand any special requests before leaving on your trip (i.e. Punta Cana you must pay a $10

❖ Some hotels have special resort fees not included in your reservation & you are expected to pay there.

HOW TO AVOID PASSPORT AND VISA PROBLEMS:

CHECK YOUR EXPIRATION DATES!

YOU CAN'T TRAVEL OUTSIDE OF THE US IF YOUR PASSPORT EXPIRES WITHIN 6 MONTHS of any of your travel dates.

For example my passport expired on May 10th, and I was traveling the prior December 7 to 18. That was within the six month window, and I had to renew my passport before I left the country.

Go to a passport photo place to make sure they take the right photo. Passport photos must meet specific requirements; if not your passport will not be issued.

Check the guidelines of countries you are planning on visiting as to what is required. If you were born in another country and are not a US citizen but living in the U.S., there are other requirements for you to be able to visit other countries. I had a client who was a Philippines citizen who wanted to go to France. He had to actually go to the French consulate here in the United States to get a special Schengen visa to enter France.

He had to fly to California as it was the only consulate that would issue this type of visa. A Schengen visa is a short-stay visa that allows a person to travel to countries of the Schengen Area for stays up to 90 days for tourism or business purposes. The Schengen visa is the most common visa for Europe. It enables its holder to enter, freely travel within, and leave the Schengen zone from any of the Schengen member countries.

For additional information please go to:
www.schengenvisainfo.com

MAKE SURE YOUR NAME
MATCHES
BOTH
YOUR PASSPORT
AND
YOUR AIRLINE TICKETS

HOW TO PACK LIGHTLY

- ❖ Put the clothes you want to bring into 3 piles must take – would like to take – not that important.

- ❖ Select a lightweight suitcase with wheels.

- ❖ Take items that don't wrinkle: cotton knits and blends, wool cashmere, 100% nylon or polyester, sweaters, denim.

- ❖ Pack only what is needed, and try to keep everything in a single, carry-on bag.

- ❖ Pick one basic color (black, grey, brown or navy), then add tops and scarves to vary your wardrobe.

- ❖ Think through what activities you will be doing, and determine what shoes and outfits will be worn.

- ❖ Roll items in your suitcase – takes up less space and will also keep your clothes from getting wrinkled.

- ❖ Essentials include toiletries, lightweight sweaters, something to read, and clothing.

- ❖ Think scarves – consider various layers you can wear.

- ❖ Don't put your address on your luggage – instead put a phone number.

- ❖ Tie a bright ribbon on your suitcase – easier to spot as it goes around the airport carousel.

- ❖ Know what the guidelines are for carry-on luggage (when measuring include the wheels and handles).

- ❖ Invest in luggage cubes which allow you to compress lots of clothes into a compact space.

- ❖ Vacuum pack it. You'd be surprised how much air is between the clothes in your suitcase(s). But beware your clothes will be very wrinkled if you use this method. Good for things you are not concerned about wrinkling.

HOW TO AVOID WRINKLED CLOTHES:

Roll, don't fold. It doesn't just save space, it can prevent wrinkles.

Don't over pack (or under pack). Wrinkling is caused when the bag is under packed or overstuffed, so add or remove items until you have the perfect amount to keep everything in place while traveling.

Many hotels offer irons in their rooms.

Purchase a wrinkle release spray product that you can pact in your check-in bag.

Don't bring anything that wrinkles easily. My entire travel wardrobe is made up of clothes that resist wrinkling.

Try steaming clothes in the bathroom.

The Most Important Thing Is To

HAVE FUN

And

MAKE MEMORIES

Meredith "KIT" Bromfield

Kit is a Travel Advisor whose main goal is to take care of all of your travel details. Her desire is for people to have fun and make memories and know that they are in good hands when they travel.

She owns Crossing Your Bridge Travel, LLC.

She has authored 16 books.

She is a speaker for Stonecroft ministries.

She loves to travel and has been all over the world.

She lived in Illinois most of her life.

She moved to Colorado in 2009 and tells everyone "living here is like being on vacation every day."

She lives in Palmer Lake with her husband.

She enjoys babysitting her 3 grandkids, reading, swimming, and hiking her beautiful Colorado Mountains.

CONTACT INFO:
KIT523@HOTMAIL.COM
WWW.CBGT.COM

www.ingramcontent.com/pod-product-compliance
Lightning Source LLC
Chambersburg PA
CBHW070811240726
48654CB00007B/298